To my mom and dad,

To my mom, a fighter in every sense of the word, whose strength and resilience have always been my anchor.

To my dad, who keeps me on my toes, challenging me, pushing me, and reminding me to never settle.

You both drive me crazy, but in the best possible way.

This book is for you.

STORIES WOVEN IN SMOKE

DANIEL EBOR CHALLAM

Made with ❤ on the Notion Press Platform
www.notionpress.com

Preface

This book was born in a time of silence and uncertainty, during the pandemic, when the world paused, and I found myself back in Shillong, far from the life I had carefully pieced together in Delhi. The sudden return to my hometown, a place both familiar and unfamiliar, was jarring — a cultural whiplash that left me feeling neither here nor there. The quiet hills seemed louder than the chaos of the city I had come to embrace. This change of pace and place forced me to confront parts of myself that I had left behind.

Yet, the seeds of this book were planted much earlier, in 2014, when I left Shillong to study and live in Delhi. In fact, a few pieces in the book, were taken from what I had written during my time in Delhi. Those years away shaped me in ways I am only now beginning to understand. The vastness and anonymity of Delhi made me look back at my roots, not with disdain or indifference, but with a newfound appreciation. I began to see Shillong for all that it was — its beauty, its traditions, and its resilience — and for all that it was becoming.

Shillong today is a city in transition, straddling modernity and tradition. Its skyline is dotted with buildings that could almost touch the clouds, yet beneath them, life still clings to the rhythms of the past. This book captures that duality, that constant negotiation between what is and what was. The hills whisper stories of belonging, but they also echo the strain of change.

Now, I live in Shillong once more, and I cannot imagine being anywhere else. The streets, the hills, the mist — they feel like pieces of a puzzle I fit into. Living here now feels like a quiet acceptance of all that I am and all that this place continues to teach me. While my years away allowed me to grow and evolve, my return has given me roots, grounding me in a way no other place ever could.

The structure of this book reflects this journey. It begins where it ends, with the first three poems in dialogue with the last three. This symmetry mirrors the circularity of life in Shillong, a place where the past is always present, and where every end is a beginning.

Inspired by the themes in one of my pieces, *Home, Again*, this collection is an exploration of what it means to belong, to leave, and to return. It is a conversation between the Shillong I left behind and the Shillong I rediscovered. It is a story told through poems — woven like smoke, transient yet enduring, capturing the ephemeral essence of home and identity.

May this book be a companion to those who have wandered, those who have returned, and those who are still searching for home.

Language

Communications
Breaking down,
Babble of tongues like
Foreign sounds;
Misunderstandings
So many,
Misinterpreted
In plenty.

Babble On (Language - Part II)

Words fall, break apart,
Many voices fill the air —
None can understand.

Ki kyntien ki pra,
Ki lyer ki dap da ki sur —
Ym don ba sngewthuh.

Wiar jingmut i ktien,
Dap ka pûrthai dei awri —
Ĭ mai wa sniawthōh?

Kattaan grijok,
Balwa gam·anian gapa —
Na·a ma·siama?

Words drift and then fade,
We grasp at what still remains —
Do we speak, or pass?

Lost in Translation (Language - Part III)

We gather words like fragile threads, weaving them into meaning,
Trying to hold the pieces together, though they crumble in our grasp.

Gather words like fragile threads, weaving them into meaning,
Trying to hold the pieces, though they crumble.

Words like fragile threads, weaving meaning,
The pieces together, though they crumble.

Like fragile threads, weaving.
Together, they crumble.

Threads, weaving,
Together, crumble.

Threads,
Crumble.

Lost.
Silence.

In Search of Solid Ground

People always ask me,
"Where are you from?",
Sometimes, I don't think much about it.
I simply tell them, "I'm from Shillong"
Because that's all I've ever known,
And possibly will ever know.

Or do I tell them, "I'm from Jwai"?
A distant past
My Grandmother's mother left behind,
In search of a fresh start;
From Durga to Shidamon,
From Durga to Christ.

Or do I tell them, "I'm from Changpung"?
Grandfather's roots
Gently tugged by love's hand -
A love not found in words,
But in a little photograph
Held onto by a loving brother in Poona.

I yearn for a space,

I can call my own;

I search and roam,

A wanderer forevermore;

In a tapestry of my mother's roots,

I return to find anchorage.

Between Hills and Highways

I come from a land where clouds drift low,
Where the air hums with whispers of ancient songs,
And the hills guard stories in their folds;
But what do these hills mean to me,
When I am not their keeper, not their kin?
When the soil clings to my shoes, but not to my spirit?

Here, belonging is a story told in circles,
Where kinship is currency,
And the collective outweighs the self;
But I, a child of concrete and iron towers,
Was not made for circles;
I walk in straight lines.

Culture has become performance,
A ribbon unspooling for an audience's applause;
Every event begins with the same choreography —
A war dance turned museum piece,
A song once sacred, now staged;
The crowd claps, and I can't help but feel nothing.

I watch as heritage is framed, boxed, priced, and sold;
What does it mean to belong to something
That only stands still for cameras?
For something that wears its skin
Only when called upon to do so?
This is not pride, it is a puppet show.

And yet, I do not belong anywhere else;
I walk through cities —
Bright lights as blinding as their indifference,
Roads like veins pumping endless motion;
My name carries the sound of my home,
But my voice belongs to no place.

I am an individual
Before I am a son of the hills,
Before I am a face in the crowd,
Before I am a name that echoes my ancestors' songs.
To the world, this makes me rootless —
To me, this is freedom.

So here I stand, between hills and highways,
The past a fading shadow, the future a question unanswered;
Perhaps belonging is not a place,
But a path I may never find,
But one I will continue to walk alone,
Until this song feels like home again.

Exile

The cherry blossoms arrive,
Pink like soft whispers
Before the frost bites;
They mark the end of autumn's fire,
And the beginning of loneliness;
Winter creeps in quietly
Like a thief in the night —
A fog rolling in, like the secrets we all keep.

People leave,
Bags heavy with sweaters, gifts, memories,
Headed to villages and hometowns
With names and histories;
They go to be warmed by hearths, by laughter,
While I stay grounded,
Tethered to a city that is mine
And yet, not.

Shillong, a city of humming wires and pulsing roads,
Becomes silent in December —
Its electricity pulled back, the lights dim,
And the energy seeps out with the sun, fading;
Replaced by a cold that nips at exposed wrists,

Creeping into my bones —
A reminder that winter is not a celebration,
But a hollowing out.

The days between Christmas and New Year,
Stretch like an endless loop —
A Limbo where each morning is the last,
And each night a copy of the one before;
Groundhog days in a city that feels
Empty, abandoned,
Waiting to come alive again in the spring,
When warmth and colour will return.

I walk the streets alone,
Feeling like an outsider;
While the fog thickens,
And the silence settles,
Here, in the emptiness I remain,
Without the homecoming.

Kjam

The day begins in stillness,
A hush before the frost awakens.

The air is khriat,
Not biting yet, but sharp enough
To make you stay close to the heater.

By ten,
The sun nudges warmth into the hills,
Its rays brushing past icy grass,
Melting the edges of dawn's frost;
The world is deceptively calm.

But by noon,
The wind stirs;
It creeps through doorways,
Whispers through pine needles,
And turns pjah water into an unkind chill;
Afternoons, cloaked in gloom,
Pull you beneath blankets,
The TV's glow, your only sun.

By evening,
The dait-thah begins,
The cold no longer shy,
It gnaws at your fingers,
Slips past woollen layers,
And settles deep into your bones;
The coal crackles loud now,
A desperate fight against the dark.

At dawn,
The frost reigns supreme,
A frozen shimmer over every blade of grass;
The world is suh-jer,
Still and silent beneath the frost's grip.

The sun lingers on the horizon,
Not yet ready to rise above the hills,
Spilling faintly into the waiting sky.

The day begins in stillness,
A hush before the frost awakens.

The Granary

Rice
Grains like tiny moons,
Spilling from sacks into the year ahead;
The staple of every table,
A foundation for feasts and survival alike.

Dal
Golden and red,
Lentils waiting to bloom in boiling water;
They carry the taste of home,
The warmth of hearth and care.

Sugar
Crystals of sweetness,
Hidden in jars like tiny treasures;
It whispers that even in lean times,
There will be moments to savour.

Salt
Silent and unseen,
But without it, the world is bland;
Its weight is humble,
Yet it binds us to the earth and to each other.

Oil
Amber and liquid light,
The flow that feeds the flame;
It readies us for the storms to come,
A quiet, shimmering shield.

Together
We fill the granary,
Not with extravagance, but with care;
As one year fades and another begins,
This ritual bridges the past and the future,
Reminding us that abundance
Is not measured in plenty,
But in preparation.

4

The bougainvillea spills in vibrant hues,
At Dhankheti — its pinks and violets, bright;
The springtime whispers promises through dews,
As fields awake to greet the seeds of light.

Beneath the jacaranda's purple skies,
Their blossoms crown the Secretariat lane;
The rivers swell, as clouds through valleys rise,
As summer paints the hills and plains with rain.

The cherry blossoms blush in golden rays,
Their fleeting beauty, surrounding Ward's Lake;
As autumn calls, the fields resound with praise,
The season's gifts, a harvest none forsake.

The me·gong blooms where warmer winters lie,
Its snowy petals gleam by Umiam's shore;
As orange trees with sweetness fill the sky,
A fleeting warmth that lingers evermore.

Shillong

Where clouds gather like old friends
And the wind carries stories of belonging;
Tell me, who can call you home?
Is it the mist that wraps around your peaks,
Or the rain that drums on tin rooftops?

Do you belong to the Khasis,
Who have known your red soil the longest,
Who speak to your rocks and streams
As if they were kin?
Your laws say yes,
But your streets hum with the steps of many.

The British left their mark too,
Reshaping you into a summer retreat,
Building wards and clubs,
Bungalows and churches;
Do you still carry them in your bones,
Or have they faded like the monsoon mist?

And the Garos, who crossed hills to build lives here;
Do they belong to you?
What of the Bengalis, Nepalis, Assamese,
And Marwari traders?
The students from Manipur, Mizoram, Nagaland?
Have they carved out corners in your heart?

Shillong, you are a crossroads,
Where traditions meet the present,
Where sacred groves stand near coffee shops,
And festivals light up the cold winter nights.
Your music reaches far,
But so do the cracks in your peace.

Do you belong to only those who own your land,
Or to those who have only walked it?
Are you a place for the rich,
Who build high walls and quiet gardens,
Or for the poor,
Who fill your bazaars with life?

Your history is restless —
A patchwork of settlers and visitors,
Colonizers and keepers,
Politicians and pressure groups,
All claiming pieces of you;
While you remain silent.

And yet, perhaps you belong
To none of them entirely;
You breathe through all who live here,
In the clamour of small town / city life,
In the stillness of your hills,
In the stories that never stop telling themselves.

Shillong, whose city are you?
Maybe you are simply yours —
To share, to shelter, to have and to hold;
A keeper of memories
Never truly owned,
Only ever belonging to time.

Mountains Move You

In the south, where the clouds gather first,
Lum Shillong rises, cloaked in mist,
A sentinel veiled in whispers;
They say U 'Lei Shyllong,
Dwells here, watching over the people;
The streams flow like lifelines,
Carving paths of memory into the hillsides;
Its presence is a quiet strength,
A reminder that protection is sometimes unseen,
Like the wind that shapes the pine trees.

To the north, where heaven meets earth,
Lum Sohpetbneng crowns the horizon;
The Navel of Heaven, they call it,
The golden bridge
That once bound mortals and gods.
Seven clans descended its sacred ladder,
Carrying stories that pulse in the Khasi heart;
Its presence is a prayer,
A hymn rising with the first light,
A connection to what is eternal.

To the west, Lum Diengïei looms,
Its flat summit bearing the weight of lore;
Once, a great tree grew here,
Its branches vast, stretching across the sky,
Enveloping the world in shadow,
Until the tree was felled —
Its mighty form cut down to free the light;
The hill now stands as a quiet witness,
A reminder of power unchecked,
Of the balance that light and shadow demand.

Whispering Pines

We grew up beneath the pines,
Their needle-like leaves stitching sunlight
Into the playgrounds of our youth;
Blotches of gold danced on our faces,
Shifting with the wind that whispered
Secrets only the trees could keep.

Our hands knew the rough touch
Of dried pine needles,
Heaps, woven into forts and walls,
Temporary kingdoms of imagination.

Pine cones became treasures and tools —
Cricket balls, mysterious seeds
With wings that promised flight;
We'd crack them open,
Pretending to find gold.

The sap, sticky and amber coloured,
Oozed like a tree's quiet blood,
Turning our mischief into art.

When the pines would shed their pollen,
Everything turned yellow —
A dusting of gold that made the mundane magical;
We'd breathe it in,
Dreaming of riches in the air,
While sneezes and allergies betrayed our fantasy;
A shimmer that settled on leaves,
On rocks,
On us.

Even now, I still smell the pine,
Sharp and earthy,
Especially when the rain
Sends its scent rising
From the forest floor.

And in the evenings,
The smoke of burning pine wood
Lingered like an old song,
A melody of warmth and familiarity;
We knew the power of its resin,
How a single twig could coax a flame
Into roaring life,
Its crackle a steady companion
On cold Shillong nights.

Now, when I see them —
The White Pines, Red Pines, English Pines,
Their tall, elegant forms swaying —
I wonder how many children
Still play in their shadows,
Still find magic in their cones,
Still shake their branches to feel
The world spill over with dust and light.

Seasons change,
But the pines remain.

U Slap

The clouds descend with quiet song,
Their shadows stretch across the hills;
It starts as whispers, soft then strong,
A rhythm that shapes this land still.

The shadows stretch across the hills,
The streets are drowned in flowing mud;
A rhythm that shapes this land still,
But crushes dreams with every flood.

The streets are drowned in flowing mud,
As rivers rise, and waters swell,
It crushes dreams with every flood,
As landslides tear through rock and shell.

As rivers rise, and waters swell,
Umbrellas snap, and roofs give way;
As landslides tear through rock and shell,
Yet farmers plead for rain to stay.

Umbrellas snap, and roofs give way,
It starts as whispers, soft then strong,
Farmers still plead for rain to stay;
The clouds descend with quiet song.

Ward's Lake

It's where we went after school,
Feeding puffed rice to the ducks
From the top of the bridge,
Watching the ripples carry our laughter.

Mornings bring joggers, pacing the curve,
Their breath mingling with the mist;
Afternoons, it's boat rides,
Pedals spinning, slicing the water clean.

Autumn turns the lake into a stage —
Poets, storytellers, music in the air;
Winter wraps it in a quieter charm,
The chill softened by Christmas lights.

We've all come here at some point,
Drawn to its calm in the city's noise,
Finding a bench beneath the shade,
Or standing still, just watching the geese.

But even as the years go by,
Ward's Lake stays the same:
A quiet escape, a moment to pause
Right in the middle of everything.

Iewduh

At the top, where the market takes its first breath,
The air is thick with feathers and clucks —
Chickens of every shade caged in bamboo;
Men, with backs bent under bundles twice their size,
Shuffle through like ants on a foraging path;
A knup sways in the breeze, a khoh cradles vegetables,
And whistles pierce the air, sharper than words;
Cutting through the crowd like invisible knives —
"Shuh!" they say, though no one listens;
Shoulders bump, arms graze,
This is the rhythm of Iewduh.

The pathways twist and spill,
Veins pulsing with people,
Each artery leading to a different part of Shillong —
Garikhana, Motphran, Police Bazar,
Each entrance whispers a promise, each exit a secret;
You could lose yourself here,
In a maze of bamboo and flesh,
In the din of barter and laughter,
A world where overflow is the only constant.

Where the crowd thickens,
A cluster of Mawbynna stands still
On a tiny patch of grass,
Surrounded by concrete walls and rising towers —
Their stoic silence a stark contrast
To the chaos that churns around them;
The weight of time, like the weight of the crowd,
But they hold their ground,
Monuments to memory.

Lower down, the market changes its tune;
Fish scales glisten like mirrors in the sun,
Their scent mingling with crushed betel leaves
And turmeric-stained hands;
Grains of perilla and sesame pour like sand through careful
fingers,
While berries, vegetables,
Kwai, and ktung pile in pyramids —
Red, Orange, Yellow, Green, Brown, and Black,
A spectrum of the earth's flavours.

But everywhere, always,
The unceasing hum of life is spilling,
Pouring over the edges,
Like the pathways themselves —
Veins without a heart,
A maze without a centre;

Iewduh breathes,
Its pulse strong,
And I, a wallflower,
Watch from the edges,
Trying not to be swept away.

Changing Skyline

It begins with bamboo,
Rising from the earth,
Bent and woven into homes of thatch and light.

The wind slips through their walls,
Carrying the scent of pine and monsoon rain,
Simple shelters, soft against the hills.

Then came the Assam-type houses,
Wooden frames, tin roofs, and plastered walls,
A middle ground—neither earth nor stone;
Bamboo holds them still,
Lending strength to fragile dreams,
Its poles a skeleton beneath skin.

Now, concrete and steel reach for the sky,
Structures of permanence and ambition;
Glass facades reflect the clouds,
Yet the bamboo scaffolding surrounds them —
A reminder that even the modern
Rests on ancient shoulders.

When the scaffolding falls away,
The bamboo returns to the earth,
Splintered, forgotten, but never absent.

It ends with bamboo,
Rising from the earth,
Ready to hold the next vision aloft.

Nuclear

The village once held us close,
Arms open, walls unseen,
Laughter echoed through the hills,
Songs carried by the wind,
Feasts for all, tears shared,
Together we mourned, together we lived.

But time moved on.

We live apart now, we mourn alone,
Tears hidden, feasts forgotten,
The wind carries silence,
Through the hills soft sobs linger,
Walls rise high, arms closed,
The village now lets us go.

Time Moves Differently Here

In Delhi,
Time roars like traffic,
A merciless Sun melting seconds into minutes;
Unrelenting, unstoppable,
A horn blaring at every red light —
Go! Go! Go!

Here in Shillong,
Time drips,
Like raindrops off tin roofs,
Sometimes steady,
Sometimes in fits and starts —
Pitter, patter, pitter, patter......

A day can feel like a week,
But a week can slip through your hands
Before you even realize it's gone.

They say U Lum Sohpetbneng once stood tall,
A golden bridge to heaven,
Until impatience broke it;
Now, patience is all that's left —
The slow rhythm of waiting

For clouds to clear,
For traffic to untangle itself,
For rain to stop;
And if it doesn't?
Oh well, there's always tomorrow......

In Delhi, time is a predator;
Deadlines chase you down,
Commutes on the metro devour your hours,
And before you can even catch your breath,
Another day has fled;
Good night!

In Shillong,
Time is an old storyteller;
It loops back on itself,
Taking the long way round each time;
It tells you the same story
Five times, ten times, a hundred times,
Changing a word or two each time;
You never mind......

Four seasons in a day —
Morning: a crisp autumn chill,
Noon: summer light spilling through pine trees,
Afternoon: monsoon's sudden rage,
Evening: winter's cold breath creeping in;

Time pirouettes, and you lose track —
Was it yesterday, or today?
Does it even matter??????

In the markets,
Women selling kwai and turmeric
Ask why you're in a hurry,
"Balei ba kyrkieh?"
Hurry? In Shillong?
That word doesn't belong here;
Sit, chew a little kwai —
The world will have to wait......

But time isn't always kind —
A slow afternoon can stretch
Into an eternity of longing;
The rain, unrelenting,
Can feel like a pause button
Pressed too long;
You start to wonder
If the sun forgot to rise at all......

Somewhere between the chaos of Delhi
And the calm of these hills,
I find myself stuck;
A pendulum swinging,
Too fast for here,

Too slow for there,
And always at the wrong place,
At the wrong time.

But then I see the mist
Curling around the hills,
Rising like smoke from a distant chimney —
Unhurried, unbothered,
Moisturized by the ever-present drizzle,
Staying in its own lane,
Thriving in its element;
And I think to myself,
Maybe time here isn't slow or fast.
It's just free.

Movement in Still Life

Shillong,
A town where the days once stretched long,
But the world doesn't wait,
And neither do the wheels.

The roads are like veins —
Narrow, winding, overwhelmed,
Meant for a trickle,
But forced to bear a flood.

They once guided bullock carts
And feet hardened by the hills,
Now clogged by dreams in chrome and rubber,
Where patience dies a slow, honking death.

The hours slip by, where moving forward
Is measured in meters per lifetime;
A journey so absurd it feels like the town itself
Is holding its breath.

And then, we have the Scootys —
Darting, swerving, overtaking sense itself;
No space too small, no gap too narrow,
If they could, they'd rise over you, crawl under you.

These are the growing pains
Of a town bursting at the seams,
Of a place that cannot expand fast enough
To fit the ambitions of its people.

So I choose to wait indoors when I can,
Sharing spaces in public taxis,
Trusting two-wheeler Rapidos;
I adjust, because Shillong cannot.

And yet, there is beauty hidden beneath the gridlock;
This town survives,
No matter how heavy the weight,
Bleeding beneath the layers of dust and exhaust.

But I wonder how much longer
Before the seams give way,
Before memories once held together by monsoons and pine,
Unravel into noise and fumes?

Traffic Symphony (Movement in Still Life – Part II)

Shillong, oh Shillong, where the honk-honks compete,
With beep-beeps and zoom-zooms, a chaotic beat;
The vroom-vrooms of Scootys go darting around,
While chug-chugging buses just grumble and frown.

The clatter and chatter of wheels on asphalt,
Mix splish-splashing puddles with rhythms that halt;
A moo from a cow, and a bark from a stray,
While screeching brakes join in the city's ballet.

The pines try to whisper, but cough-cough, they choke,
Exhausts spiral up like a mischievous joke;
The clouds go drip-drop on the roofs down below,
But sizzle on cars while the engines still glow.

The ka-thunk of potholes, the ding-ding of bells,
The whoosh of a wind that gets lost in the smells;
For Shillong's alive with its cacophony,
A riddle in traffic, a loud symphony.

Piat

The outermost layer,
Thin, papery, flaking at the touch,
Hides the heart of a humble vegetable;
In the market, it piles high,
A pearl of earth and pungency,
Filling baskets and kitchen shelves —
The constant, in every cuisine.

The next layer bites back,
Crisp and raw,
A spicy apple that stings the tongue,
And the eyes;
Sharp and bold,
Carving its place in every dish,
Every gathering, every conversation.

Another layer, softened by flame,
Sweats gently in butter or oil,
Its sharpness fading into sweetness,
A golden transformation;
Now it whispers, not shouts,
Blending into syrwa and sboh,
Bringing depth without seeking attention.

Peel further, deeper,
And you find the social butterfly,
The friend who lights up a room —
Yet beneath all that charm,
Other layers await,
Layers of silence, longing, and truth
Hidden from the casual gaze.

The innermost layer,
Holds the essence
Of what it means to be whole;
Even when peeled and dissected,
The onion remains a mystery;
Its layers endless,
Its core never fully revealed.

And so,
We return to the onion, to piat,
A vegetable,
A metaphor;
A reminder that
There is more to people,
Than meets the eye.

Lost, then Found

The books I gather hold what once was lost,
Their pages whisp'ring stories we forgot;
They crossed the seas, they landed on strange coasts,
To bring them home has been my only thought.

Their pages whisp'ring stories we forgot,
Of lives and lands these writers never knew;
To bring them home has been my only thought,
A thread connecting past to present view.

Of lives and lands these writers never knew,
Their echoes live within this sacred space;
A thread connecting past to present view,
These books come home to claim their rightful place.

Their echoes live within this sacred space,
They crossed the seas, they landed on strange coasts;
These books come home to claim their rightful place,
The books I gather hold what once was lost.

Notes on a Hill Tribe People: Blackout Reflections from P. R. T. Gurdon's The Khasis

Frequently attached,
Fond of nature —
Love a day out in the woods;
Thoroughly enjoy fishing,
Content to sit still,
And contemplate nature —
A separate name
For birds and flowers,
Butterflies and moths,
Traits not found usually.

Not above manual labour —
Quite ready to take the hoe,
In his potato garden;
Excellent stonemason, carpenter,
Ready to learn fancy mechanical work.

Inveterate chewer
Of supari and pan leaf,
Distances often measured
By the number of betel-nuts chewed on a journey.

Spirit distilled
From rice, millet;
Rice beer used
For ceremonial purposes,
Spirit inhabitants of the high plateaux
Content to partake of
A good deal.

But it must be remembered that
People excel,
For they
Speak the truth
As a rule —
Simple and straightforward.

This blackout poem was created using page 5 of: Gurdon,
P. R. T. (1914). *The Khasis*. Macmillan and Co. Ltd.

frequently   attached
fond of nature.
love a day out in the woods,   thoroughly enjoy
fishing,   con-
tent to sit still and contemplate nature.   a separate
name for   birds and flowers.
butterflies and moths.   traits
not found usually
not above manual labour,
quite ready to take   the hoe
in his potato garden.   excellent stonemason
and carpenter   ready to learn fancy
mechanical work.   inveterate chewer of supari and
pan leaf
distances   often measured
by the number of betel-nuts   chewed on a
journey.
spirit distilled from rice
millet. Rice beer   used
for ceremonial purposes. Spirit
inhabitants of the high plateaux
content to partake of
a good deal   but it must be remem-
bered that
people   excel, for they   speak the
truth
as a rule, simple and straightforward

Notes on a Hill Tribe People: A Second Look

Frequently attached,
Bound deeply to the pulse of life,
Fond of nature —
They love a day out in the woods,
Where the air carries whispers of leaves;
They thoroughly enjoy fishing,
Casting lines into flowing waters,
Content to sit still,
Lost in thought,
And contemplating nature —
A separate name,
A language unspoken,
For birds and flowers,
Butterflies and moths,
Traits not found usually
In the haste of the world.

Not above manual labour —
Quite ready to take the hoe,
Calloused hands working the soil
In his potato garden;
An excellent stonemason,

Shaping the bones of the earth,
A carpenter building dreams in wood,
Ever ready to learn the secrets
Of fancy mechanical work.

An inveterate chewer
Of supari and pan leaf,
Distances often measured
By the rhythm of jaws,
By the number of betel-nuts chewed
On a journey that stretches
Through hills and horizons.

Spirit distilled
From rice, millet;
Rice beer — sacred, shared,
Used for ceremonial purposes,
An offering and a comfort;
Spirit inhabitants of the high plateaux,
Quietly enduring,
Content to partake of
A good deal,
Their laughter carried
On the winds of tradition.

But it must be remembered that,

Despite simplicity,

These people excel,

For they

Speak the truth,

As a rule —

Their words are simple

And their hearts

Straightforward,

Clear as mountain streams,

Unclouded and enduring.

Nongkyndong

I come from one of the
Corners of the world,
Where clouds knit shawls for the hills
And rivers hum their ancient ballads;
They call me Nongkyndong —
As if to say, "You are untouched,
Unformed, unfit for the light
Beyond your narrow sky".

But what they don't see,
What they don't know,
Is the way curiosity stirs like a restless wind
Inside those of us who
Come from the edges;
How we stare at horizons,
Not with fear,
But with wonder.

Yes, I have been that child,
Feet calloused by red earth,
Unfamiliar with the languages
Of city walls and concrete skies;
And I have been that stranger,

In the bustling streets of Delhi,
Where the air smelled
Of ambition and alienation.

I could have clung to the familiar,
Woven my tongue tightly
Around my mother's words;
Found solace only in those
Who spoke my name without stuttering;
Defended the smell of my food,
As if its pungent truth
Needed an apology.

But —
I also chose to taste the sharpness
Of foreign spices,
To walk into rooms
Where my silence felt heavier
Than my speech,
To let discomfort carve
New spaces in my soul.

Call me Nongkyndong,
If it means I carry my roots
Like a lucky charm,
Not an anchor;
If it means my ignorance

Is not a boundary,
But the beginning of
A map waiting to be drawn.

I will take your cities, your books,
Your stories, your cuisines, and your chaos,
Fold them gently into myself
Like a sacred offering;
I will return to the hearth
And feed them to the flame,
Let their warmth mingle with
The ferment of bamboo shoot.

For what is a villager,
But someone who knows
The wildness of home
And still hungers to taste the world?
What is a Nongkyndong,
But a heart unafraid
To leave the corners
And chase infinity?

3

Three stones hold the fire,
Steady, unshaken, complete;
The heart of the home.

Three mothers gave life,
Root, branch, and leaf intertwined;
An eternal line.

Three pillars uphold:
Mother, uncle, and daughter;
Roots that bind us all.

Three paths interweave:
Father, Son, Spirit above;
Iing, kur, jaitbynriew.

Three duties define:
Righteousness, reverence, kin;
The circle stays whole.

Three voices call still,
The hills, the streams, and the skies;
Harmony persists.

Three realms guide the soul,
The living, spirits, divine;
Paths we tread with care.

Three days keep the wake,
Doors open, hymns rise, tears fall;
Farewell shared as one.

Three, not a number,
But rhythm, balance, and truth;
The way of the world.

7

Seven days, the wheel of time,
Seven tribes, a lineage prime;
Seven huts, a tale to thread,
Seven sins, where paths are tread;
Seven roots, the choices made,
Seven marks both faith and fate;
Seven turns of love and loss.

Carrying

At dawn,
She bends under the weight of water
Cradled against her hip;
Her steps steady on the worn path,
Carrying the day's first task.

But she carries more than water —
She carries bundles of grass,
Firewood stacked on her back;
Arms strong from gathering, from lifting,
From gathering and lifting.

She carries the harvest of her labour,
Their colours bright against the earth —
Anger kept quiet, love sown deep,
Regret for all that can't be changed,
And courage to hold onto hope.

In her body, she has carried life,
The silent months of waiting,
The slow work of creating
Something out of nothing;
The first cries of a newborn.

Beyond flesh and bone,
She carries what can't be seen:
The legacy of lineage, the weight of a household,
The knowledge of seasons, seeds, and soil,
Of family and place, of means and ends.

She holds the delicate balance
Of all that is hers to keep,
Passed down by mothers who came before,
And daughters who will follow —
The memories of generations etched in her bones.

She carries the earth in her spirit,
Knowing her place is here,
Where her hands have shaped,
And will shape
The land that answers only to her name.

This is the art of carrying —
All that lies below, above, and within;
Carried forward, step by step,
For those who will come,
And carry it in turn.

A Mother's Weave

She is the loom —
Quiet, steady,
Weaving strength into softness;
Each thread a promise,
Binding warmth to patience,
Binding love to the air between breaths;
The shawl she gives you is not just silk —
It is her.

Her hands are the forest,
Dipping into earthen hues,
Pulling colours from roots and leaves;
Her voice hums in the fibres,
The thickened lines she carves into the weave
Are her wards —
Shields against shadows
That fall where her arms cannot reach.

Her embrace is worn close —
Soft against your shoulders,
Strong enough to keep the cold away;
The shawl remembers every path you've walked,
Every tear, every wind;

It does not fray,
It does not falter,
Just as she does not.

Even when you leave,
You carry her with you,
Draped over you,
A quiet presence in the folds of cloth;
And when you return,
The shawl, like her arms,
Opens wide again,
Always warm, always home.

Kamra Shetja

In the Kamra Shetja, the fire crackles gently, its orange glow spilling across the darkened room, where walls, stained black with soot, bear the marks of countless meals and memories. Three stones, the Mawbyrsiew, hold the flames steady, a sacred triangle where pots rest and life begins. Fire is no ordinary force here. She is the youngest Daughter of Ramew, Mother Nature, and Basa, the village's guardian spirit. Like the youngest Daughter in matrilineal Khasi homes, she tends to the household, bound by duty and love. If she were the eldest, like the Sun and Moon, she would roam freely, leaving a trail of destruction behind. But her place is here, in the hearth, nurturing life and binding kin together.

Flames dance on the stones,
Nurturer and destroyer —
Her warmth tames the dark.

The kitchen is more than walls and utensils. It is the heart of the home, where rice bubbles in pots and the air carries the scent of turmeric and smoke. The youngest Daughter, inheritor of hearth, clan, and property, knows her role. She stirs the rice, whispers to the fire, keeps the lineage alive.

In the flicker of flames, the stories of ancestors emerge —
voices of those who once sat by this very hearth.

But sometimes,
She looks at the soot-stained walls and wonders —
Is this her destiny, or a cage?
Bound by tradition, praised for her role,
Yet the weight of inheritance feels like chains;
She envies the fire's dance, its fleeting sparks,
Knowing she too, could blaze.

Smoke rises, curling —
Ancestral whispers linger,
Woven with the wind.

Fire, like the youngest Daughter, has her limits. She must be
tended, coaxed, and tempered. Left to wander, she devours
all in her path. The mawbyrsiew ground her, much like
tradition tethers the family. Fire embodies balance — she
nourishes, but she can consume.

But unlike the youngest Daughter, Fire dreams of wandering
— of breaking free from the Mawbyrsiew's tether, of writing
her own story. Yet, she knows her absence would leave
destruction in her wake, unravelling the order she was
meant to protect. Like the youngest Daughter, she is both
feared and needed.

Her embers breathe slow,
Holding both love and ruin —
A fragile rhythm.

In Khasi matriliny, the youngest Daughter is the custodian of the home, the hearth, ancestral property; the weight of continuity. Through her, the clan endures. Like Fire, she is the quiet keeper of life's rhythm, bound by duty but glowing with purpose. In the Kamra Shetja, Fire and Daughter are one: both protectors of the hearth, both tied to the eternal cycle of care, even as both long to blaze their own trails.

Flames flicker softly —
The hearth a sacred altar,
Time held in her hands.

Fire and Daughter (Kamra Shetja - Part II)

Fire:
Born of Ramew's breath,
I cradle pots, warming life,
Yet forests fear me.

Daughter:
Tied to Kamra Shet,
Inheritance weighs on me,
I dream of elsewhere.

Fire:
I boil your rice soft,
Crackling songs of ancestors,
Yet stones keep me bound.

Daughter:
I stir the lineage,
Stories flicker in my hands,
Tradition holds tight.

Fire:
If eldest I were,
I would roam like Sun and Moon,
Leaving ash behind.

Daughter:
If eldest I were,
The wind would carry my name,
Far from this tether.

Fire:
Three stones anchor me,
Sacred mawbyrsiew's balance—
Duty, warmth, and care.

Daughter:
I too am held fast;
Kur, kin, clan — three bonds that bind,
Circle unbroken.

Fire:
Together we burn,
The rhythm of hearth and home,
Protecting the heart.

Daughter:
Together we stand,
Kamra Shetja's quiet guards,
Where warmth births love's flame.

Both:
Bound, yet we endure—
The keeper and the kept one,
Flame and nurturer.

Red & Gold

The coral beads of the Paila,
Warm and deep, like the earth's pulse,
Threads of velvet, the colour of life;
Red whispers of strength,
Of love unbroken,
Of fire that sustains and consumes.

The solid gleam of hammered beads,
Bright and enduring, like the sun's blessing;
Gold shimmers with promises kept,
Of wealth, of faith,
Of light that guides
Even in the longest night.

Together they sing —
The past and the present,
Tradition and celebration,
The pulse of the people —
Weaving through silk Jainsems;
The warmth of Christmas —
In Khasi homes, on Christmas trees;
Red and Gold hold hands —
Life and light, a bond eternal.

Ode to 'Tiew Knupmawiang

In quiet woods where sunlight softly falls,
The Lady Slipper blooms, both rare and bright;
Its petals curve like tiny cradled walls,
A fleeting wonder, hidden from plain sight.

My mother held you on her wedding day,
A bloom of love, so delicate, so true;
You marked her joy in such a simple way,
A moment held in time, a perfect view.

You call the hills your home, the clouds your shade,
Your roots in stories told through mist and rain;
A beauty built to last, yet bound to fade,
Both here and gone, a joy we can't explain.

Forever blooming, quiet and unseen,
A humble queen in forests lush and green.

Ode to 'La Basa

Clouded hunter, silent grace,
Haunts the hills with shadowed face;
Who could shape your rare design,
Trace each spot with art divine?

What great hand could craft your form,
Soft as mist and swift as storm?
Who could weave the clouds that show
On your coat, their ghostly glow?

What wild heart, both fierce and still,
Drives you through the forest's will?
What keen eyes, so sharp, so bright,
Pierce the secrets of the night?

Do you tread where gods reside,
Fleeting form of might and pride?
Does your shadow mark the way,
Blessings cast in light of day?

Do the trees bow as you pass,
Whisp'ring tales through leaves and grass?
Do the winds, in quiet song,
Guide the path where you belong?

Clouded hunter, soft and rare,
Born to move through earth and air;
Who could dream a soul like you,
Wild and free, forever true?

Ode to Moina

A shadow split the sky,
Its feathers black and sleek,
It soared above the sacred hills,
Its call, both clear and meek.

It landed on a tree,
Its golden beak aglow,
And mimicked words from voices heard,
A song from high and low.

The trees began to sway,
Their leaves began to hum,
As if the forest leaned to hear
The words from which it'd come.

O Moina, wild and free,
What secrets do you share?
Do you bring blessings from the groves
Or whispers from the air?
You vanish with the breeze,
Shadows against the sky,
And leave behind a melody,
A hymn that cannot die.

'Tiew Rakot's Lament

In forests deep, they call me cruel, unkind,
Devourer hiding in the shadowed green;
My curves they say, are traps to snare the blind,
A monster shaped for hunger — sharp and keen;
They see my form and whisper tales of fear,
But is survival such a crime, my dear?

I am no demon, only alive.

The winds repeat their stories, harsh and plain,
Of prey that falls into my waiting jaws;
But do they see the roots that drink the rain,
Or wonder how I live without a cause?
I grow where barren soil will never yield,
Where life depends on balance to survive;
Each insect feeds the earth, each drop I steal
Becomes the reason other roots can thrive.

I am no demon, only alive.

Look closer now, and see what I provide,
The veins that trace my story, strong yet frail;
I'm no deceiver, thief, or wretched guide,
But proof that even hardship can prevail;
Don't call me cruel, for I am nature's hand —
A fleeting gift within this ancient land.

I am no demon, only alive.

Dukan Sha

In a dukan sha, the hearth is always warm,
The kong presides with grace, her steady hand;
Through fire and rain, they carry the same charm.

The early mist retreats, the day takes form,
While smoky tea brews softly as she planned;
In a dukan sha, the hearth is always warm.

Umbrellas drip, a shelter from the storm,
Yet laughter fills the room, a lively band;
Through fire and rain, they carry the same charm.

The scent of rice and curry will transform
This humble space into a homely stand;
In a dukan sha, the hearth is always warm.

No throne, no crown, no rank can outperform,
Where all are equals, seated hand in hand;
Through fire and rain, they carry the same charm.
At night, the glowing embers still perform,
Their warmth, a light for those who need a hand;
In a dukan sha, the hearth is always warm,
Through fire and rain, they carry the same charm.

Sha Saw

Oh, Red Tea,
Amber liquid of comfort,
Piping hot in porcelain cups,
You greet the weary at dawn,
And bid the day farewell at dusk;
No visitor leaves unwelcomed,
No moment truly begins or ends
Without your gentle presence.

You are simplicity steeped in ritual,
Unadorned, no milk, no sugar,
Yet rich as the hills that cradle you;
From the dpei of Khasi homes,
To the infinite tea stalls
Dotting winding highways;
You are a constant,
A bridge between strangers and friends.

Your steam rises,
Carrying the whispers
Of a thousand sunlit mornings,
The chatter of dukan sha,
Where truckers pause and villagers linger,

Hands wrapped around glasses,
Voices mingling
With the hum of the road.

And oh, the act of dipping —
Jingbam wieh sha, food to meet the tea;
Pumaloi, Tpusaiñ, Sakin,
Or the unconventional and absurd;
Whatever the hand holds,
It finds its way to you,
A habit born of memory,
Of generations steeped in your warmth.

Even the air bends to your scent —
Bitter, earthy, smoky awakening;
You are the pause, the comfort,
The silent companion after a long day;
You are not just tea,
You are culture brewed to perfection,
A ritual passed from hand to hand,
From the hills to the highways.

Oh, Red Tea,
You go by many names —
Sha Saw, Cha So,
Cha Gitchak, Lal Chai,
And so on.....

You are the heartbeat of our days,
The thread that binds our lives,
One steaming cup at a time.

Feast

Upon the table,
A feast both simple and rich,
Flavours fill the plate.

In homes beneath the tall pines,
The fire's warmth unites us all.

Beyond these borders,
Laws dictate what's pure to eat,
What lives are sacred.

But hunger does not ask why,
Nor bow to the will of men.

History lingers;
A single bite lights the spark
That splits a people.

Yet here we gather,
Rites of blood and kinship shared,
Each taste defiant.

The hill winds whisper,
"Eat what nourishes your soul,
And let no man judge."

Rice

Rice is more than food —
It is life,
It is soil made edible,
It is the rhythm of our days;
No meal begins without it,
No hunger truly ends;
It fills our bowls,
But also our stories,
Our songs,
And our rituals.

From the terraces of the Khasi hills,
To the damp fields of Jaintia valleys,
To the lowlands where Garo hands toil,
Rice is sowed, cherished, harvested —
A circle of life
Repeated with reverence,
Nurtured by sun and rain,
A grain earned,
A grain blessed;
The foundation of a feast.

We eat it as it is,
Steamed and fragrant;
Or transformed —
Into Putharo, flat and humble,
Into Pudoh, rich with pork,
Into Sakin, layered with sweetness
And the dark whispers of black sesame;
It is fried into Pukhleiñ,
Or stirred into a Pura gravy,
A quiet thickening, a binding.

Rice is also spirit —
It ferments into Kyad Um,
Bubbles into Minil Bitchi,
Flows into celebrations
Running from dusk till dawn;
It loosens tongues,
Brings laughter to the harvest,
And warmth to cold nights;
Turning labour into joy,
And tradition into communion.

And yet, rice is also power;
A handful scattered in rituals —
The naming of a child,
Or the binding of a curse;
It carries weight beyond its grains,

A vessel for unseen forces,
A bridge between the everyday
And the sacred,
Weaving through the mystical
And the mundane.

It is white,
The canvas for every flavour;
It is sticky,
Holding families together;
It is red,
Stained with the colour of soil;
It is black,
Rich as the velvet night sky;
It is Joha,
Fragrant as the first rains of the summer.

Rice is what we are made of —
Our flesh, our bones, our spirits;
It is not merely sustenance,
It is identity,
It is our harvests;
To live without rice
Would be to live without land,
Without roots, without memory;
It is our past, our present,
Our offering to the future.

Salt

Salt,
The quiet keeper of flavour,
Hidden in the heart of every meal,
Its absence louder than a gong;
What is a broth without it,
Or rice, or meat, or wild greens?
Even the simplest fare —
Boiled roots and foraged leaves,
Transcends with a pinch,
Becoming something whole,
Something human.

Salt is universal,
Woven into the fabric of our tongues —
We call it Mluh in Khasi, Blooh in Pnar,
Kari in Garo, Namak in Hindi;
The syllables change,
But the truth remains:
Salt unites —
In our sweat,
In the sting of tears,
In the boundless oceans
Caressing the Earth.

Salt carries history —
Journeys on caravans,
Glitter in tribal feasts,
It rests in clay pots
Passed down
Like whispered secrets;
It crosses borders,
Where language falters,
Reminding us that hunger
Has no nation,
Only the longing to be whole.

And yet, salt does not only nourish,
It protects;
Sprinkled across thresholds,
It holds the line
Between the seen and unseen;
A ward against harm,
A binding element in rituals
Older than memory;
Salt knows the weight of the sacred,
Its grains scattered like
A map of the stars.

Where would the world be
Without salt?
A tasteless, spiritless shadow
Of itself;
Salt is the alchemy of life,
The first blessing,
A quiet hymn
To all that sustains us,
Drawing us together,
One grain
At a time.

Fermentation

In the quiet embrace of earthen jars and leaves,
Time whispers secrets to humble ingredients —
Soybeans become Tungrymbai,
Dried fish transforms into Tungtap,
Sticky rice surrenders to the alchemy of Kyad.

Through the patient work of unseen hands,
Flavors deepen, the sour becomes savoury,
Textures evolve, the sharp becomes mellow,
The raw and the wild mature into the profound,
And what was once repelled, now invites.

This is how life works too, right?
Our experiences, left to steep in reflection,
Ferment into wisdom;
The sharp edges of youth soften,
Yielding a richness that only time can bestow.

Like kimchi resting beneath its fiery cloak,
Or rum cake absorbing spirits in darkened cellars,
I think of the waiting, the patience;
We are all, in our own ways,
Becoming.

Embrace the wait,
Trust in the unseen ferment;
We are all like the foods we cherish,
Better with time —
Each choice, each hurt, each love,
Left to mature in the quiet,
Until one day,
We taste of the earth,
Of fire,
And of time itself.

Bamboo Shoot

You gifted me
A jar of bamboo shoot —
Said it needed time
To ferment,
To grow,
To taste better with time.

But that was over
A year ago......
Things have soured since then;
And we've been falling
Out of touch.

I still have your jar of bamboo shoot,
It just sits there,
Unopened,
Still fermenting;
I wonder,
Does it taste any good now?

Would it,
If I dared to try?

Spirits

In the hills, they sip Kyad and Chu,
A brew for the many, not few;
In joy or in pain,
It falls like the rain,
Traditions both ancient and new.

In villages, jars overflow,
At the hearth where warm fires glow;
A drink to unite,
By day or by night,
Its strength helps the spirits to grow.

For weddings, they toast with Kyad sweet,
In mourning, Chu's bitter notes meet;
It binds every heart,
Plays its quiet part,
A solace where joy and grief greet.

Though the world builds walls and divides,
Kyad and Chu cross where love resides;
A bond to restore,
A link to the lore,
Of the hills where the spirits abide.

Klong

A gourd stood gentle — smooth and round,
It's hollowed form both strong and sound;
Shaped with love and care,
For drinks it would bear,
In rituals where spirits abound.

The gourd, with its neck long and thin,
Holds stories of what lies within;
It pours out the past,
Like ladles held fast,
A vessel for life to begin.

The short-necked ones, sacred and bright,
Are homes where the spirits alight;
They carry the sound
Of whispers around,
And gleam in the stillness of night.

I hold them with joy in my hand,
Each form, a story time has planned;
Its curves tell a tale,
Through time's endless trail,
A relic both humble and grand.

U Siej

Bamboo rises, humble and unyielding, from the embrace of red earth. Its hollow stems are whispers of resilience, bending but never breaking. Once, it stood as the backbone of thatched huts, walls that sang with the wind, floors that felt the rhythm of bare feet. Now, it scaffolds dreams of concrete and steel, a quiet supporter of modern ambitions.

Green stalks in the breeze,
Holding up the weight of hope,
Silent, steadfast roots.

Artisans see more than a plant; they see a muse. Knups that shield faces from monsoon's kiss, khohs cradling the harvest, spoons shaped to stir memories into pots. Every fibre carries a story, every weave a prayer. Its versatility transcends craft — it is jewellery, it is song, it is survival.

Hands weaving bamboo,
Threads of culture intertwined,
Craft becomes life's breath.

In the hearth, bamboo transforms again. Shoots tender and tangy ferment into flavours that linger, leaves become fodder for the wild and tame. Even in death, it nourishes, its ashes returning to the soil it sprang from. Nothing is wasted; everything is given.

Flavors of the earth,
Tangy whispers on the tongue,
A gift for all life.

Pressed and pulped, bamboo bears the weight of words. It holds history in its veins, fragile yet enduring, a keeper of memory in scrolls and books. Its stories are etched in time, its legacy carried forward by human hands.

Fragile veins of leaves,
Carrying the weight of words,
A story preserved.

Bamboo is the lifeline of these hills, weaving life, and tradition into one tapestry. It grows endlessly, returning always to the earth it calls home. In its cycle of giving, it reminds us of the balance between strength and surrender, of life's quiet persistence.

Rising from the earth,
Returning in endless loops,
Bamboo holds the world.

Kwai

Host's hands offer it
The blood-red heart of culture —
Shikyntien Kwai speaks.

A nut, a leaf, and lime, bond,
In its folds, old ties revive.

No one is greater,
No one less — chewing as one,
We share one flavour.

In weddings, funerals too,
It whispers: "We all belong."

"Bam Kwai ha dwar Blei,"
They say — at heavn's gates we share,
Our final moment.....

Crimson-stained mouths chew—
Kwai offered with open hands,
Kwai speaks for us all.

The Wake

Three days and nights,
The house remains open —
Its doors, its windows
An invitation to the unseen,
To the spirit of the departed —
To wander,
To linger,
To say goodbye.

Inside, white lace curtains frame the body,
A figure now at rest
Yet surrounded by life;
This is a practice we have kept,
Carried through the years,
Unchanged — not relic, but root,
Grounding us in who we are,
Even as faith transformed.

Around the room,
Family and friends gather;
Voices weave stories
Into the fabric of grief—
Not to erase it,

But to hold it,
To soften its edges
With laughter, with memory.

At night, games are played,
Carrom boards echo with clicks and slides,
Teacups clink softly,
And kwai is passed hand to hand —
The nut, the leaf, the lime,
Marking all mouths red
As if to say,
"We are together in this loss."

On the third day,
The community swells —
Faces arrive from distant places,
Each bearing their own grief,
Their own offerings of love;
The scent of turmeric and pork cooking,
The sound of plastic chairs shifting,
Voices rising in solemn hymns.

The burial begins,
A final farewell not in silence,
But in the hum of voices;
Death here is not lonely —
A thread pulled tight between the living
And those who have gone before,
A reminder that no one,
Is ever truly alone.

To Remember is to Carry Stone

To kynmaw is to carve in stone,
And leave a mark when voices fade;
To remember is to carry stone,
A lasting bond through time we've made.

To leave a mark when voices fade,
The earth will hold what we impart;
A lasting bond through time we've made,
Each stone a tale etched in our hearts.

The earth will hold what we impart,
Not lightly, nor as fleeting breath;
Each stone a tale etched in our hearts,
A voice enduring after death.

Not lightly, nor as fleeting breath,
To kynmaw is to carve in stone;
A voice enduring after death,
To remember is to carry stone.

Home, Again

I've always called Shillong home —
Eighteen years of childhood
(Fifteen of those were school),
Walking the same streets,
Breathing the same pine-soaked air,
Watching the landscape rise and fall,
Rise then fall,
Like old companions.

The first time I left,
It felt like tearing,
Like roots pulled out of soil too soon;
College in Delhi —
Six years of learning
Not just from books,
But from the rhythm of a city
That never stopped moving.

I tried to keep up;
I built a home there,
Piece by piece—
A couch I chose myself,
Plates I washed after late dinners,

Shelves that held way more books than they should have;
It felt like permanence,
Until it wasn't.

The pandemic came like a storm,
Sweeping me back to Shillong,
To streets I had stopped calling mine;
I remember the first few months,
The silence of lockdowns louder
Than the city's usual quiet;
Everything the same,
And yet, it was all so unfamiliar.

It felt like exile, at first —
Missing the chaos of Delhi,
Missing the life I'd built;
But slowly, the hills worked their way back —
The mornings began to speak,
The evenings softened around me,
The air carried stories I'd forgotten,
Memories hidden in the cracks of these old hills.

Now, I live here again,
Not as the teen who left,
But as someone who has returned,
To relearn what home can be;
Delhi is a chapter,

One I'll always revisit,
Maybe one of many other chapters;
But Shillong is the book.

It holds me in a way no other place could —
Not always gentle,
Not always kind,
But steady, like roots
That know the soil they belong to;
Yes, I know it's complicated,
Yes, I know it's imperfect,
Yes, I know it's flawed.

And yes, it's home.

Found in Translation (Language - Part IV)

Silence.

A word.

Threads,
Grow.

Threads, meaning,
Together, grow.

Fragile threads, forming meaning,
Pieces together, they start to grow.

Words like fragile threads, forming meaning,
Holding the pieces together, they start to grow whole.

Gather words like fragile threads, forming them into meaning,
Holding the pieces together, they start to grow whole, in our grasp.

We gather words like fragile threads, weaving and forming them into meaning,
Finding strength, holding the pieces together, they start to grow whole, mended in our grasp.

Still Babbling On (Language - Part V)

Words weave into form,
The air begins to clear now;
Meaning finds its way.

Ki ktien ki wan dur,
Ym don shuh ka jingkulmar;
Baroh ngi sngewthuh.

Da wan dur ki ktien,
Ûm em de i jingkulmar;
Waroh da sniawthōh.

Katta ong·baa,
Gimaa uigijani;
Pilakan ma·sia.

Voices rise as one,
A harmony long unseen;
Noise gives way to peace.

Tapestry

Many voices rise in this sacred place,
Each carrying histories time cannot erase;
Garo, Khasi, Jaintia — names that resound,
Holding stories, but they're not the only sound;
Across these hills, others walk with pride —
Lives of Hajong, Rabha, Koch, cannot hide,
Ancestors of Boro, Karbi, Biate too,
Yearning for recognition, for what is due;
All are threads in this tapestry we weave.

Glossary Of Terms And Phrases

Balei ba kyrkieh? – Khasi for 'why in a hurry?'

Bam Kwai ha dwar Blei – Khasi for 'chewing betelnut at heaven's gates.'

Basa – Khasi tutelary deity of the village.

Blooh, kari, mluh – Pnar, Garo and Khasi terms for 'salt.'

Cha gitchak, cha so, sha saw – Garo, Pnar, and Khasi terms for 'red tea' or black tea.

Changpung / Shangpung – Village in West Jaintia Hills, Meghalaya

Chu, kyad – Garo and Khasi terms for 'alcohol.'

Dait-thah, khriat, kjam, pjah, suh-jer – Different ways to say 'cold' in Khasi and Pnar.

Dhankheti – Neighbourhood in Shillong, Meghalaya. Assamese for 'rice field.'

Dpei – Khasi for 'hearth.'

Dukan sha – Khasi for 'tea shop.'

Garikhana – Neighbourhood in Shillong, Meghalaya.

Iewduh – Largest traditional market in Shillong, Meghalaya.

Iing – Khasi for 'home' or 'house.'

Jainsem – Traditional Khasi attire worn by women.

Jaitbynriew – The Khasi race.

Jingbam wieh sha – Khasi for 'food to dip in tea.'

Joha – Variety of rice widely cultivated in Garo Hills, Meghalaya and Assam.

Jwai / Jowai – District Headquarters of West Jaintia Hills, Meghalaya.

Kamra Shetja – Khasi for 'kitchen.'

Khoh – Khasi conical basket used for carrying items.

Klong – Khasi or Pnar for 'bottle gourd.'

Knup – Khasi umbrella worn over the head, covering the back, shaped like a teardrop.

Kong – Khasi or Pnar honorific to respectfully address a woman.

Ktung – Khasi for 'dried fish.'

Kur – Khasi for 'clan.'

Kyad um, minil bitchi – Khasi and Garo terms for 'sticky rice wine'.

Kynmaw – Khasi for 'to remember.'

'La Basa – Khasi for 'clouded leopard.'

'Lei Shyllong – The name of a Khasi God, after whom Shillong is named.

Lum Diengïei – Hill to the northwest of Shillong, Meghalaya, where it was believed that a tree grew, which covered the Earth and shrouded it in darkness.

Lum Sohpetbneng – Hill to the north of Shillong, Meghalaya, believed to be the 'navel of the universe.'

Mawbynna – Khasi megaliths and monoliths.

Mawbyrsiew – Khasi for three stones set in the hearth between which fire is kindled.

Me·gong – Garo for flower of bauhinia variegata.

Moina – Khasi for 'hill myna.'

Motphran – Neighbourhood in Shillong, Meghalaya. In Khasi, it translates to 'monument of France.'

Nongkyndong – Khasi for 'villager.'

Paila – Coral and Gold necklace worn by Khasi and Jaintia men and women.

Piat – Khasi for 'onion.'

Pudoh – Khasi sticky rice balls filled with meat.

Pukhlein – Khasi fried sticky rice cake.

Pura – Garo gravy made using rice flour.

Putharo, Tpu-sain – Khasi or Jaintia flat rice cake.

Ramew – Khasi for 'Mother Nature'.

Sakin – Garo layered rice cake with black sesame.

Sboh – Khasi for 'gravy.'

Sha – Khasi for 'tea.'

Shikyntien – Khasi for 'a mouthful.'

Siej – Khasi for 'bamboo.'

Slap – Khasi for 'rain.'

Syrwa – Khasi for 'broth.'

'Tiew Knupmawiang – Khasi for 'lady slipper orchid.'

'Tiew Rakot – Khasi for 'pitcher plant.'

Tungrymbai – Khasi fermented soybean paste.

Tungtap – Khasi fermented fish paste.

U – Khasi pronoun for 'he / him.'

Umiam – Lake north of Shillong, Meghalaya.

Translations From Babble On (language - Part Ii) And Still Babbling On (language – Part V)

Khasi:

Ki kyntien ki pra,
Ki lyer ki dap da ki sur —
Ym don ba sngewthuh.

(Words they crumble,
The winds are filled with voices —
No one understands.)

Ki ktien ki wan dur,
Ym don shuh ka jingkulmar;
Baroh ngi sngewthuh.

(Words they take form,
There is no more chaos;
We all understand.)

Pnar:

Wiar jingmut i ktien,
Dap ka pûrthai dei awri —
Ï mai wa sniawthōh?

(Words they lose meaning,

The world is filled with quarrel —

Who will understand?)

Da wan dur ki ktien,

Ûm em de i jingkulmar;

Waroh da sniawthōh.

(Words they take form,

There is no more chaos;

We all understand.)

Garo:

Kattaan grijok,

Balwa gam·anian gapa —

Na·a ma·siama?

(Words lose meaning,

The air is full of noise—

Do you know?)

Katta ong·baa,

Gimaa uigijani;

Pilakan ma·sia.

(Words become,

Ignorance disappears;

Everyone knows.)

I would like to express my gratitude to Samanda N. Pyngrope, Betsame Lamar, Chiangkle G. Momin, Keenan K. Marak, and Jarim R. Marak for their invaluable help with the translations. Your support and expertise have been truly appreciated.

www.ingramcontent.com/pod-product-compliance
Lightning Source LLC
Chambersburg PA
CBHW031304130726
47988CB00007B/2717